Original title:
Beneath the Thicket

Copyright © 2025 Creative Arts Management OÜ
All rights reserved.

Author: Oliver Bennett
ISBN HARDBACK: 978-1-80567-420-7
ISBN PAPERBACK: 978-1-80567-719-2

The Hidden Harvest

In the bushes, the veggies lurk,
Chubby carrots pretending to work.
Tomatoes giggle, so red and round,
While sneaky cucumbers hide in the ground.

Salad greens dance, oh what a sight,
As radishes play tag, full of delight.
But watch your step, they trip and fall,
Those crafty plants are having a ball!

Under leafy roofs, the laughter grows,
With peas in pods wearing silly clothes.
Zucchini racing on tiny wheels,
Making a ruckus, oh how it appeals!

So if you wander where veggies meet,
Don't miss the show—it's quite a feat!
For in this garden, the fun won't quit,
The harvest here is a comedic hit!

Beneath the Aging Boughs

In a tree so old, it tells a joke,
Squirrels gather, ready to poke.
They chatter about nuts, quite the feast,
Planning a party, to say the least.

Branches swing low with a creaky sound,
While creatures below dance round and round.
A wise owl hoots, a comical sight,
Winks at the dancers, and ignites the night.

The Quiet Symphony of Growth

The worms wiggle, the ants march proud,
Under the moss, they form a crowd.
Grass blades giggle as they reach for the sun,
Nature's orchestra has just begun.

A bumblebee trips over its own wings,
While flowers chuckle at the joy it brings.
Each raindrop falls with a ploppy tune,
Nature's humor blossoms, morning to noon.

Secrets from the Shade

A toad sits still, a minus one frog,
Stakeout mode set, it's stuck like a log.
With a fly up close, it makes its plan,
But misses the mark; oh, what a fan!

The grass blades giggle at the sight so keen,
As the toad shakes off its sticky sheen.
In the shade, secrets travel fast,
Witty whispers shared, none quite the last.

A Tapestry of Leaf and Loam

Cornered by roots, a worm tries to hide,
Tangled in leaves, with nowhere to glide.
It twirls and twists as the wind gives a shove,
In nature's dance, it cries, 'Where's the love?'

The loam chuckles with a crumbly grin,
As the weathered stones can't help but spin.
With laughter in the air, the forest unveils,
A patchwork of humor, where nature prevails.

Underneath the Canopy

Squirrels put on quite the show,
Chasing tails and dodging low.
They trip and tumble, what a sight,
In this game of morning light.

The branches dance with giggles high,
While shadows cast a silly lie.
A rabbit's hop, a snail's slow creep,
Nature's laughter, secrets to keep.

Whispers Among the Leaves

The leaves gossip with the breeze,
Sharing tales of puddles and bees.
A grasshopper croaks with endless cheer,
While mushrooms chuckle, loud and clear.

Birds in hats, oh what a sight,
They strut and preen until the night.
The breeze winks, it knows the score,
Tales of the forest, always more.

The Lurking Light

A firefly with a silly grin,
Plays hide and seek, let's all join in.
It flickers and darts, a glowing tease,
Before landing softly on a sneeze.

The moon looks down, a giggling fool,
As owls hoot from their leafy school.
Mice in capes, what a grand parade,
The night-time antics never fade.

Veiled in Verdancy

Frogs in tuxedos, what a show,
Jumping and croaking, 'Look at me now!'
In a patch of green, they stage a play,
With dragonflies buzzing, "Hip Hip Hooray!"

The bushes make a rustling sound,
As a hedgehog rolls with grace unbound.
Nature's laughter fills the air,
In this hidden world, fun is everywhere.

The Canopy's Cry

In the shade where squirrels plot,
A raccoon bids, "I'll take that slot!"
The branches shake with giggles bright,
As owls roll eyes in pure delight.

The jays take turns with loudest squawks,
While ants parade in tiny frocks.
A tumbleweed rolls, round and round,
Spewing laughter, such a sound!

The saplings sway, joining the fun,
It seems the sun has just begun.
The tree trunks smile in the warm breeze,
A party held among the leaves.

What mischief brews in nature's core,
With every rustle, hear them roar!
The canopy's alive and well,
In this leafy, laughing shell.

Laughter in the Leaves

Up above, the branches jig,
A dance that makes the robins gig.
The sunbeams poke, as if to tease,
The laughter spills between the trees.

A fox jumps high on mushroom cap,
While beetles share a cozy nap.
The shadows play their funny tricks,
As nature whispers silly blips.

With acorns bouncing off the ground,
The critters gather from around.
A chorus of chirps, a joyful spree,
In this land of glee and jubilee.

Swing low, sweet branches, swing high,
For every sigh, a snappy fly.
Laughter bubbles, crickets chirp,
In leafy realms, we twist and burp.

Under the Hushed Branches

With every flutter of a wing,
A secret whispered, then takes wing.
The shadows hold a chuckle tight,
As fawns jump high, a silly sight.

The thorns all giggle, quite the prank,
While turtles smile along the bank.
Each rustle tells a silly tale,
While frogs don tiny, leafy veils.

The breeze teases the hanging vines,
With tug-of-war that intertwines.
A porcupine wears prickly shoes,
As laughter bursts with morning hues.

What fun it is to play and jest,
In nature's arms, we find our rest.
Beneath the shade, a raucous cheer,
With every giggle, joy is near.

Depths of the Overhanging

In tangled roots, the critters jest,
With hedgehogs dressed as pirates, best!
A squirrel with swagger, thump and clap,
Creating chaos on the map.

The mushrooms jabber, share a laugh,
While snails debate the perfect path.
A lopsided grin on caterpillar's face,
As leaves join in this lively race.

The wildflowers giggle in the sun,
Flirting with bees on the run.
A flicker of wings, a plump little bee,
Whirring through plants with no decree.

With every tickle and rustling sound,
The depths hold joy that knows no bound.
In this thriving, uproarious mass,
Nature rejoices, letting time pass.

Drowned in the Moss

A frog jumped high with a splashy cheer,
Landing right where the ground's soggy, oh dear!
His croak turned to giggles, a slippery dance,
With each little leap, he took quite a chance.

In laughter, he found his green soggy throne,
While snails noticed, oh how they'd groan!
They stuck to their shells, sharing tales quite tall,
Of frogs with a penchant for slip 'n' fall!

Embrace of the Twilight

At dusk, the critters all come out to play,
Chasing shadows till they ran away.
A squirrel mistook a branch for a swing,
Now he's dizzy, that must be something!

The fireflies twinkled like stars on a spree,
Buzzing around as if giddy with glee.
Silly bugs joined in a glowing ballet,
In the twilight, the ruckus holds sway!

Lured by the Understory

A hedgehog wandered, all fluffy and round,
Seduced by a snack that he just couldn't find.
He rolled in the leaves, a comical sight,
Lured by the scent of a feast he'd delight.

In pursuit of a berry, he took quite the spin,
Spilling some seeds, oh where to begin!
His friends rolled around in a dance of a chase,
Each leaf they dislodged brought a smile to their face.

The Curl of the Vines

Vines twisted 'round the silly old tree,
A dancing pair in a leafy jubilee.
The wind started chuckling, a playful tease,
As branches waved back like they're saying, "Hey, freeze!"

A squirrel took notice, with eyes full of mirth,
He joined in the fun, giving roots a good girth.
Together they swayed, in their earthy attire,
Becoming a chorus of nature's silly choir!

Hidden Canopy

In the shade where squirrels play,
They hide their acorns every day.
A sneaky fox, with a cheeky grin,
Tries to chase his tail, but can't begin.

A raccoon steals a snack from a tree,
While the owls hoot, "Look at me!"
A parade of ants march through the grass,
Each one thinking they're the first in class.

The branches sway with laughter bold,
As stories of the woodland unfold.
The buzz of bees, a comical sound,
As they trip on flowers, tumbling down.

Underneath this leafy spree,
Nature's circus is plain to see.
With clumsy critters and giggly songs,
The laughter here forever belongs.

Whispers in the Underbrush

Whispers dance among the leaves,
Where funny secrets the critters weave.
The chipmunks gossip about the crow,
While the frogs leap high, putting on a show.

The hedgehogs roll, all spiky and round,
Trying to hide, but they've been found.
A turtle tries to race and slip,
But ends up in a leaf pile trip.

A turtle, slow, meets a hare, so spry,
"You can't outrun me!" the turtle sly.
They settle for a snack, both agree,
That munching leaves is the best spree.

Laughs echo in the tangled green,
As nature's jesters are often seen.
In this riotous patch full of cheer,
Life's a joke — just grab a beer!

Secrets of the Woodland Floor

Underfoot where secrets creep,
The funny mushrooms start to peep.
Mice with hats in a tiny parade,
Whispering tales of the plans they made.

A snail on stilts makes his way,
Saying slow and steady wins the day.
But the kangaroo rat is quick and spry,
Jumping over him with a twinkle in his eye.

The shadows play a silly game,
As leaves fall like confetti, what a fame!
Beneath the ferns, a party's set,
Where all the critters have no regret.

In the thicket, laughter soars,
With woodland friends behind closed doors.
The woodland floor's a comical maze,
A riot of humor that forever stays.

Shadows Among the Roots

Shadows offer a cozy seat,
With roots that twist and little feet.
A badger hums a tune so bright,
While a beetle tap dances in delight.

The moles start telling jokes galore,
While squirrels argue who sees more.
Beneath the roots where giggles thrive,
They munch on berries, oh how they jive.

A wise old owl hoots a punchline steep,
"Why did the tree take a nap? It was deep!"
The laughter spreads through leafy glades,
As autumn's humor never fades.

In hallowed shade, the antics roll,
With creatures gathered, heart and soul.
Nature hides its joy in the gloom,
With shadows that dance and brightly bloom.

Threads of the Untamed

In the jungle, a squirrel prances,
Wearing acorns like bold little pants.
A raccoon dances, a hat on his head,
While wise owls chuckle, with laughter they've fed.

The vines twist and turn, a tangled parade,
Where vines play hopscotch in the sun's bright glade.
A chattering monkey swings high, oh so spry,
With a cheery "banana!" echoing nearby.

Grasshoppers snap to a jazzy beat,
Twirling round, making nature feel sweet.
A snail joins the fun, all slugs in attendance,
Together they shimmy in slimy abundance.

Under the canopy, chaos prevails,
Where each creature shares their outrageous tales.
In this nutty forest, laughter's the rule,
And silliness reigns; the wild is our school.

Starlit Secrets

In the moonlight, shadows take flight,
A hedgehog in shades looks quite a sight.
With a wink and a nod, he starts dancing,
While crickets applaud, their choruses prancing.

A firefly buzzes, a twinkle on loop,
Joining in rhythm with the rest of the troop.
A raccoon thief sneaks a gourmet snack,
His sticky little paws return with a clack.

Bats perform acrobatics above the trees,
While owls ponder jokes in a soft, wise breeze.
Whispers of mischief float through the air,
As skunks prance around without any care.

In this curious realm where wonders collide,
Each nocturnal pal takes life in their stride.
Secrets abound in the shadows that flicker,
As laughter and fun grow just a bit thicker.

Breath of the Underbrush

In the thicket, frogs croak with flair,
In rubbery boots, they leap through the air.
A lizard in sunglasses struts on the ground,
With every step echoing a snap of a sound.

Beneath tangled roots, ants hold a race,
With tiny helmets all on their face.
They zoom through the leaves, teamwork their theme,
While a turtle remarks, "This is not what I dreamed!"

A playful chipmunk throws nuts like a pro,
Chasing behind him, a curious crow.
With scrambles and tumbles, both giggle and clash,
As the sun shines down on their friendly bash.

In this playful haven where antics abound,
Nature's a circus; they're all quite renowned.
With laughter and joy, no worries held tight,
In this wild little world, it's all pure delight.

Hidden Hues of Nature

Among the flowers, a badger resides,
In bright polka-dot shorts, he truly abides.
With a grin on his face, he shows off his hat,
To the giggling fox, who's totally phat.

A butterfly jives in a colorful spin,
While ladybugs cheer, "Oh, let's do this again!"
The daisies all sway, forming a chain,
Singing sweet songs with joy to sustain.

Beneath leafy covers, squirrels sell jokes,
A raccoon joins in with a few clever pokes.
With laughter and grins, they joke and they play,
As the sun paints their world in a colorful display.

In this playful garden of giggles and cheer,
Where whimsy is plenty, and fun's always near.
Nature swirls bright in hues bold and grand,
As friendships bloom lovely in this enchanted land.

Unseen Paths

In tangled brush, a squirrel doth dart,
Finding snacks, it plays the part.
With acorn hats and cheeky prance,
It winks at trees, like they're in on the dance.

A rabbit hops, with ears like sails,
Tail flicks sharply, never fails.
Dodging shadows, it takes a chance,
On hidden trails, it starts to prance.

A fox trots in, with a sly old grin,
Telling tales of the things he's seen.
With a flick of his tail, oh so grand,
He finds the snacks that squirrels planned.

Everything under branches seems neat,
But no one knows they've got two left feet.
The creatures chuckle, it's all quite fun,
In this wild place where mischief's begun.

A World in Shade

In shadows thick, the mischief brews,
Where sunbeam dances and giggles ensue.
The ants are holding a tiny parade,
Marching in single file with a fruit confade.

A bear in a hat tries to bow and slip,
Bumping into trees, oh what a trip!
With berries stuck to his fuzzy face,
He laughs it off—such a clumsy grace.

Behind the ferns, a lizard lays,
Counting the toads in a hopping craze.
"Two hops for the lucky, and three for the shy!"
He chuckles softly as crickets sigh.

And when the sun dips, the laughter swells,
With owls hooting tales of woodland spells.
The shade grows deep, yet spirits climb,
This world of giggles, forever in rhyme.

In the Wake of Wanderers

Footprints scurry through leaves so green,
Poking fun at where they've been.
Each critter laughs with little claps,
As wanderers weave through grassy laps.

A turtle's slow like a rolling stone,
While butterflies tease in a playful tone.
"Catch me if you can! It's a race, you see?"
But the turtle just smiles, "I'll get there, whee!"

A raccoon on a quest for tasty treats,
Wags its tail while it slyly beats.
With mischief in mind, it shuffles ahead,
Stumbling past roots like it's lost instead.

As night creeps in, the friends all cheer,
Celebrating every silly fear.
The wanderers laugh at the paths they roam,
Content in the wild, they feel at home.

The Watchful Wild

In the heart of trees, secrets abound,
Where the funny faces of nature are found.
With critters peeking from their leafy beds,
Sticking out tongues and shaking their heads.

A wise old owl with spectacles round,
Surveys the chaos, never a sound.
"Remember kids, don't play on the path,
Or you may find the consequence—my math!"

In the underbrush, the hedgehog snickers,
As a snail races past doing quick little flickers.
"Too slow! Too slow!" the hedgehog jeers,
As the snail rolls forward, quelling fears.

The wild winks, alive with quirks,
In laughter and antics, it subtly works.
Under the canopy, life takes its flight,
In the watchful wild, oh what a delight!

Where the Ferns Embrace

In the deep of green, they dance and twirl,
A ladybug plots, with a crafty whirl.
Ferns sway and giggle, tickling the air,
While a snail brags loudly, "I'm the ruler fair!"

Frogs croak jokes no one can quite get,
A toad rolls his eyes, "It's not a safe bet!"
They hop and leap, with grand ambition,
In this jungle gym, they form a new mission!

A caterpillar munches on a leafy snack,
"Where's the party?" cries a beetle on track.
Just a brief wander, then off to explore,
In this leafy palace, there's always more!

With roots that dig deep and laughter that flows,
A hidden comedy where nobody knows.
Each twist and turn holds a surprise, you see,
In the fern's tight embrace, we're all wild and free!

The Life That Lurks Below

Worms in a meeting, plotting the day,
"Who's going to pop up, see what's underway?"
They wriggle and giggle, not one bit shy,
While ants just roll their eyes and sigh!

A mole comes waltzing, fancy as can be,
With a top hat and cane, he shouts, "Look at me!"
The ground shakes laughter as they cheer him on,
In this underground rave, from dusk until dawn!

A downy seed drops, saying, "I'm the star!"
"You're just a snack!" says a chipmunk from far.
Yet life underground is wild and grand,
With jokes in the roots, and wonders unplanned!

So let's dig deep where the funny things dwell,
In burrows and tunnels where the stories swell.
Life lurking below's a riotous show,
With whiskers and chuckles, the laughter will flow!

Veins of the Ancient Grove

In tangled branches, big whispers unfold,
A wise old oak says, "Stories are gold!"
Squirrels debate who built the best nest,
While mushrooms giggle at their lofty jest!

A raccoon strolls by with a cap and a cane,
"Look at my collection!" he calls with disdain.
He shows off a button he found in a stream,
"This is my treasure, my whimsical dream!"

Under leaves old, there's a gathering tight,
Crickets perform as the stars twinkle bright.
Each racquet of laughter gives echoes a lift,
In the veins of the grove, there's chuckles and gifts!

With roots intertwined and stories in play,
The ancient grove's tales have much to convey.
A symphony of giggles under the sky,
Where legends and laughter effortlessly fly!

Shelter of Petals and Hides

In the bloom's embrace, a bug plays a tune,
With petals as drums, he dances by noon.
Ladybugs cheer in their polka dot best,
While bumblebees buzz about a grand fest!

A flower fairy flits with a snicker and sigh,
"I've got glitter blooms, just look how they fly!"
Grasshoppers chirp, saying, "Is this even real?"
In this shelter of joy, it's all about zeal!

Dew drops are giggling, rolling down leaves,
And the flower roots whisper behind them like thieves.
In a shady nook, a dandelion grins,
"Let's scatter the seeds, let's see who wins!"

So join the parade in this blossom-filled hide,
Where nature's comedians take life in their stride.
Each petal a stage, each leaf a new line,
In this vibrant spectacle, all the world shines!

In the Foliage's Fold

Squirrels sneak snacks in leafy arms,
While ants march on in snappy charms.
A rabbit jigs with a sprightly twist,
As butterflies swirl in a sunflower fist.

The hedgehog's laughter rocks the trees,
With raccoons joining, buzzing with glee.
A parrot squawks a silly tune,
While llamas dance 'neath the bright full moon.

Here lies a secret, the critters declare,
In the shade, there's giggles floating in air.
A sloth tells jokes, with a grin so wide,
While bees hum sweetly, all full of pride.

So if you wander to playful glades,
Prepare for chuckles and silly parades.
In the green embrace, where the fun takes hold,
Life's a comedy act, in nature's fold.

Creep of the Fog

Fog rolls in, like a great gray ghost,
It tickles the toes and loves to boast.
A sly fox tiptoes, with eyes so bright,
Chasing shadows in the dim light.

A wise old owl blinks with surprise,
As dainty deer trip with graceful ties.
The misty dance brings giggles near,
While all critters chuckle, devoid of fear.

What's that? A tree branch wobbles and sways,
A raccoon insists it's just a phase.
"Don't be alarmed, it's just me," it beams,
Playing tricks in the fog's wild dreams.

So venture through where the laughter rings,
Past the hidden paths where humor sings.
In a world made of clouds, let your heart be free,
For mind-whooping antics await, trust me!

Bound by the Briars

Beneath the brambles, critters conspire,
A jumbled meeting of feline choir.
Cats with their purrs and ruffled fur,
Spotted a rat, oh what a stir!

The bunnies giggle, tripping on thorns,
While hedgehogs discuss their fancy adorns.
A crow caws loudly, "Stop with the fuss!"
Everyone wonders, "What's all the fuss?"

In the tangled vines, a strike of a pose,
A shy little mole with a nose that glows.
"Hey, I'm not lost, just pondering fate!"
The others just laugh, "Well, isn't that great?"

So if you wander where brambles might snag,
Envision a party, a joyful ragtag.
For nature's embrace can be quite a prize,
With all its comedies just waiting to rise.

Beyond the Thickening

Over yonder, where shadows stretch wide,
A turtle donned boots, and oh, what a ride!
With a wink and a grin, it speeds past a hare,
"Catch me if you can!" in a wild flank flare.

Bushy tails twirl in a verdant swirl,
While frogs launch a band, their songs in a whirl.
The badgers groove, beneath pillow soft grass,
In this jungle of fun, who needs the past?

A crow in a hat caws, "Let's flex our game!"
While squirrels engage in a nutty acclaim.
"Who's the fastest?" the children declare,
With laughter exploding – a wonderful scare!

So roam through the lands, where whimsy is king,
In a world that's alive with the joy of spring.
Beyond the dense green, pure merriment flows,
With every new step, an adventure just glows.

Of Thorns and Ferns

In the bush where prickers play,
A squirrel trips in a clumsy way,
He hops and skips, but oh, what luck!
His tail's a banner of chaos, struck!

The ferns wave gossip to the breeze,
While sneaky bugs plan their misdeeds,
A beetle boasts of grand parades,
But slips and falls in leaf cascades!

A tortoise dreams of speedy fame,
As rabbits giggle at his name,
'Fastest in the wild,' they shout,
While he just snores and rolls about!

The thorns envy the ferns so green,
'Why can't we share their lovely sheen?'
But prickles prance, they strut, they shine,
In this wild space, they're feeling fine!

Cradled by the Brush

A dandy fox with fashion flair,
Adorns his tail like debonair,
With checkered leaves and flowered bows,
He prances proud, striking a pose!

The bushes sway with whispered chats,
About the latest styles of hats,
A raccoon in a pot, oh dear!
He claims it's haute, but we just cheer!

A hedgehog rolls with joyful pride,
Unraveling secrets he can't hide,
'It's a spa day!', he cheers aloud,
As thorns applaud him, oh so proud!

And so they play in tangled bliss,
In their world, who needs a miss?
With laughter shared among the leaves,
It's a party, where nobody grieves!

The Hidden Tapestry

In the wild, a secret art,
A tapestry that plays its part,
With petals sewn by nature's hand,
And stitches made from grains of sand.

A mouse with dreams of opera fame,
Tries to serenade a passing flame,
But only manages a squeaky note,
The fireflies all seem to gloat!

A snail with bling on every shell,
Says, 'Look at me! I'm doing well!'
While others simply look perplexed,
Their fashion sense has been hexed!

They dance in loops through shadowy trails,
Crafting stories like curious tales,
As nature weaves her funny threads,
Life's a jolly show, where laughter spreads!

Nature's Labyrinth

In the maze where shadows creep,
A ladybug sings herself to sleep,
Her lullaby's a tickle and tease,
While grasshoppers dance with utmost ease!

A lost toad hops with fervent zest,
Guided by his optimism quest,
He thinks he's found the path to fame,
But trips on roots that play a game!

The hedgehogs giggle, gathering round,
To crown the toad who can't be found,
'The king of lost!' they cheer and shout,
But he just snores and rolls about!

In this wild maze, where giggles reign,
Each twist and turn adds to the gain,
For every critter shares a laugh,
In nature's maze, they find their path!

The Quiet Encroachment

In a patch of leaves so thick,
A raccoon made a fancy pick.
He donned a hat, oh so wide,
And danced with birds, with worms as his guide.

A squirrel watched from the tree,
With popcorn, he did disagree.
"That's not the style we embrace,
Let's keep it simple, not a race!"

Then came a snail with a grand plan,
To start a conga line, what a span!
But they all slipped and fell in goo,
Laughter sparked, as fun ensued!

Under twinkling lights of dew,
Creatures laughed, oh what a view!
In the chaos of a thicket mad,
Joyful moments, never bad!

Moss-Laden Secrets

In shadows moss makes a home,
Where frogs wear crowns and admit to roam.
They sing sweet songs, high-pitched and grand,
While raccoons jive, in a band so unplanned.

A sly old tortoise, quite sage in ways,
Claims he saw mushrooms with dancing rays.
"They winked at me and stole my hat!"
The crowd erupted, "Oh, imagine that!"

From acorns fell a rain of glee,
As laughter rang from the tallest tree.
The critters danced around in fun,
As stories grew in the warm, bright sun.

In a hidden glen, where fun unfurls,
A secret world of giggling swirls.
With raucous joy beneath the green,
Moss-laden tales, forever seen!

Echoes of the Burrowing Path

Down the burrowing path, with boisterous cheer,
A mole rehearsed for a show career.
He wore bright boots and a sparkly tie,
And sang to the worms, who laid a sly eye.

A hedgehog burst through, with a trumpet loud,
"Join my band!" he called, feeling proud.
"Don't worry, it's just a rehearsal spree,
With enough snacks, it'll be a jubilee!"

All the critters gathered near,
To witness a mole's debut here.
But when he slipped on patchy clay,
They roared with laughter, as night turned to day!

Yet still they cheered for the show to go on,
With worms in tuxedos, the fun had begun.
In the echoes of night, they sang with mirth,
Celebrating their quirks, down to the earth!

The Enchanted Undergrowth

In the enchanted growth, not far from the shade,
A grasshopper dreamt, while playing charade.
With leafy crowns and smiles so wide,
He jived like a pop star, full of pride.

A ladybug burst in, with sparkle and glide,
"Join me for tea, on a magical ride!"
But the captain, a snail, was stuck in a scrunch,
"You can't hurry greatness, I'll join at the lunch!"

The foliage giggled; the flowers did sway,
As they concocted a plan for the day.
Then suddenly, from underneath, came a shout,
A mole exclaimed, "Did someone bring out sprouts?"

With veggies around, they feasted with glee,
A banquet for all, 'neath the old mossy tree.
In laughter and joy, they danced till the night,
In enchanted moments, spirits took flight!

Dappled Dreams

In shadows where fairies take flight,
Squirrels debate who runs faster, quite a sight.
Crickets play tunes that tickle the ears,
While rabbits wage war with giggles and cheers.

A raccoon slips on a banana peel,
Lands in a puddle, oh what a squeal!
Birds laugh at the chaos, chirping so sweet,
As a hedgehog practices a clumsy ballet feat.

Mice throw a party, hats made of grass,
Jiving and jiggling, oh what a class!
The sun peeks in, tickling noses and tails,
While laughter and merriment dance on the trails.

In this bright glade where oddities roam,
All creatures gather, feeling right at home.
For who needs a castle or grand golden throne,
When joy and absurdity are fully grown?

Hidden in the Green

In the bushes, a secret is known,
A turtle is stuck in a half-eaten cone.
With ants as her audience, she gives a sigh,
While a nearby butterfly laughs as it flies by.

Over in shadows, a raccoon dons shades,
Pretending he's cool as he rummages blades.
He claims he's a superstar, the best of the best,
But tripping on grass? That's part of his jest!

A hedgehog rolls disco on mossy old logs,
Shaking his spines to the beat of the frogs.
Dancing through clovers, all sweet and serene,
Makes us all wonder what else could be seen.

In this lush haven of giggles and cheer,
Every minute spent here feels like a year.
For nature's oddities and woodland frolics,
Bring smiles and laughter, and never just colics.

The Grove's Embrace

In the grove, a party waits underneath,
Where bugs juggle acorns, quite a feat!
The butterflies paint their wings in a swirl,
As somewhat confused snails dance in a twirl.

Little frogs debate the finest of flies,
While a lazy old cat naps with closed eyes.
His dreams are of chasing the sun on a beam,
Unaware he'll wake up to an oddball team.

And just by the brook, a goat tells a tale,
Of chasing its shadow like a fluffy old mail.
It trips on a stone, then snickers with glee,
For laughter is shared, it's wild as can be.

So come take a wander, get lost in the fun,
Where everyone's silly and wild as they run.
With smiles all around and joy in the air,
In this hidden haven, no worries, no cares.

Echoes of Forgotten Paths

In whispers of paths long lost to time,
A hedgehog recites rhymes that rhyme.
With a toad as his fan, they giggle and grin,
At the tales of the days when he danced with a spin.

A squirrel mistook a tall tree for a stage,
Leaps in mid-air while trying to engage.
But he lands in a bush with a comical flair,
And laughter erupts with woodland's good care.

In patches of sunlight, the chipmunks all cheer,
Playing tag where the thickets are clear.
But watch out for brambles, they may not be sweet,
When you trip on their roots, they'll laugh at your feet!

So wander through echoes where fun never ends,
In each twist and turn, the laughter transcends.
For in this realm of jest and delight,
Every creature is silly, making day into night.

Beneath the Gnarled Embrace

A squirrel in a cap, what a sight!
Chasing his tail, oh, what a delight.
With acorns in hand, he belts out a tune,
While the raccoons plot under the light of the moon.

Under twisty branches with a face so wide,
The trees gossip low, seeking a ride.
They snicker and crack, share rumors of shade,
While a lost little bug, in confusion, is made.

A drumming woodpecker sings silly songs,
As rabbits rehearse their hopping along.
The laughter erupts from each creature nearby,
For even the tree frogs are learning to fly.

From this tangled place, joy leaps and spins,
Where giggles grow tall like the thorns and the sins.
A carnival thrives in the grove's twisted jest,
Which critters call home, and are always impressed.

The Cradle of Fungus and Fern

Mushrooms in hats hold a tea party so neat,
While ferns dance along in soft, gentle beat.
The snails bring the snacks, with a trail made of gold,
And toadstools debate on the stories they've told.

The bugs strut around with their fanciest wings,
While beetles recite all the joy that life brings.
With fungi as pillows, they lounge and they snack,
Laughing at shadows that tiptoe and crack.

A line of odd critters strut forth in style,
With roly-polies gleefully rolling a mile.
Each leaf is a stage for their quirky display,
As sunbeams play tricks upon this grand play.

In whispers of laughter, the garden's alive,
In a cradle of chaos, where giggles arrive.
So come join the party, don't miss the fun,
There's joy in the chaos and smiles for everyone.

Chronicles of Rooted Whispers

The roots have a secret, they whisper quite low,
A tale of the critters that prance in the glow.
Old oak chuckles soft, with its bark all a-knit,
As nutty chipmunks argue over their wit.

With tiny feet patting upon earthy floors,
The rhymes of the roots echo, opening doors.
They sing of the mornings wrapped tight in a quilt,
Where shadows play hide-and-seek, laughter is spilt.

A worm pens the tales in a journal of mud,
Observing the jam sessions right after a flood.
The frogs croak the notes, keeping time with a beat,
While fireflies flicker, tap dancing on feet.

In the softness of dusk, when the laughter is vine,
Each rustle and giggle is a hint and a sign.
As roots join the fun, tangled joy circulates,
In chronicles bold, where whimsy awaits.

Light's Dance through the Dappled Shade

Little beams of sunlight prance cheerfully round,
Planting pockets of joy on the moss-covered ground.
Dancing shadows play tag with the leaves in the breeze,
While the ants host a gala to feed the tall trees.

The dappled shade chuckles, a mischievous crowd,
As squirrels drop acorns and giggle out loud.
With flickering fireflies, they light up the night,
Making lantern-lit dance floors, a shimmering sight.

Laughter erupts from the grasshoppers' cheer,
As the caterpillars wiggle, loud and clear.
A picnic of critters meets under the stars,
With stories that travel on the wind from afar.

From morning till dusk, in this playful brigade,
Life's simple and silly in the soft, dappled shade.
Giggling and twirling, every creature partakes,
In the joy of the forest, where fun never breaks.

Tangles of the Earthbound Soul

In a jumble of socks, the gnomes did hide,
Laughing at shoes that were mismatched and wide.
A squirrel on a mission, a nut on the run,
Chasing his dreams, oh, what silly fun!

Underneath roots where the wild things dare,
A frog with a top hat, with style to spare.
He croaks all the gossip with flair and a wink,
While beetles discuss how the roses all stink.

Twisting and turning, the vines made a scene,
A dance floor for insects, oh, what could it mean?
The grasshoppers chirp while the fireflies glow,
A party of nature – come join the show!

With each funny creature, the laughter still swells,
In the tangled-up world where the mischief compels.
So join in the jolly, let your worries take flight,
In the thicket of laughter, everything's alright!

Beneath the Weaving Branches

A hedgehog in slippers strolled under the pines,
While raccoons had brunch with some cookies and wines.
They chuckle and snicker at the world as they munch,
As the badgers all join in for a wobbly lunch.

Overhead owls hoot, they have jokes to relay,
Why did the chicken cross? An age-old cliché!
The branches above sway, they're laughing away,
Echoing giggles of the woodland ballet.

A fox in a jacket is planning a scheme,
To steal all the goodies, oh, what a dream!
With a wink and a nod, he plots with delight,
It's a caper of chaos, under shimmering light.

So dance with the critters, from dawn until dusk,
In the weaving of branches, we banter and bask.
For life in the thickets is never too bleak,
When laughter is free and the fun seems to peak!

A Journey through Forgotten Greenery

On a path made of pebbles and whispers of grass,
Tiny trolls caper and raise quite a sass.
Chasing each other where the ferns intertwine,
They trip in their laughter, their mischief divine.

A parade of the nuts in their dapper attire,
Acorns in tuxedos, all ready to sire.
Each step leads to giggles, as hedges conspire,
To trip up the clowns like a prankster's choir.

Clouds peek through branches, all fluffy and bright,
While raccoon imitations clasp fingers so tight.
The whispers of breezes give puff to the tale,
Of creatures emerging from under the veil.

So journey with joy, where the laughter does swell,
In forgotten greenery, all stories excel.
For hidden adventures in silliness reign,
In the heart of the forest, there's never a pain!

Depths of the Leafy Veil

In the depths of the leaves, where the giggles grow free,
A mole sings a chorus, quite off-key, you see.
His friends in the thickets all cover their ears,
While breaking out laughing, they share in their cheers.

A butterfly flutters, with colors galore,
Buzzing around like a child at a store.
With each swirl and twirl, the ruckus is fine,
While ladybugs join in, with a sip of sweet wine.

Beneath brambles and bushes, the tales they create,
Of mischief and folly, come join in their fate.
Squirrels tell secrets that twist and delight,
Under leaves so leafy, all treasures ignite.

So dive into laughter, let joy be your guide,
In the depths of the veil where the fun can't subside.
For each crack and each crevice is bursting with glee,
In the realm of the quirky, come dance wild and free!

Life Among the Twisted Vines

In tangled trails where laughter grows,
A squirrel juggles acorns in a row.
The rabbits gossip, fluff and fur,
While dancing bees begin to stir.

Frogs play chess on lily pads,
While ants parade in silly fads.
A tortoise moves, then takes a nap,
As birds exchange their latest flap.

The sunlight spills like honeyed glee,
On every leaf and buzzing bee.
The whispers of the trees combine,
In joyful chaos, oh how divine!

Yet when the moon gives way to night,
The raccoons scheme, oh what a sight!
They steal the snacks from woodland picnics,
And laugh at all our silly cynics.

Twilight in the Green Alcove

When dusk arrives, the shadows play,
A hedgehog trips and rolls away.
The crickets tune their evening song,
A melody that can't be wrong.

The owls hoot 'bout a silly dream,
While fireflies flicker, bright they beam.
A raccoon munches on a pie,
Clumsily winking an eye.

The mushrooms dance, they sway and bend,
Their polka moves can make you grin.
As laughter echoes through the trees,
The laughter mingles with the breeze.

But if you glance at shadows near,
You might find a fox with no fear.
He plays the tricks, he pulls the pranks,
While dancing proudly on the banks.

Mysteries of the Forest Underbelly

In the undergrowth where we all roam,
A porcupine makes quite the home.
With quills like swords, he guards his stash,
Of acorns hidden in a flash.

The sleepy sloth drags on his snack,
While ants form chains in tiny packs.
A worm recites a wiggly tale,
Of rainy days and wind-filled gales.

There's laughter whispered in the muck,
As clumsy critters run amok.
A badger snorts and trips on roots,
While telling tales of clever hoots.

When nighttime falls, the jesters rise,
With shadows creeping, oh what a surprise!
The secrets held beneath the green,
Are funnier than they might have seemed.

The Subtle Breath of Leaves

The leaves converse in cheeky tones,
A plantain speaks while cracking bones.
The breezes giggle, deftly tease,
As the branches sway with subtle ease.

A mouse adorns a leafy crown,
While hedgehogs trundle through the brown.
The flowers bloom in bright parade,
Unruly blooms, no plans are made.

The squirrels play a silly game,
Of hopscotch, much to their acclaim.
A lizard takes a daring jump,
And lands on foliage with a plump.

At dusk, the trees tell funny tales,
Of wanderers with curious trails.
They chuckle soft in twilight's glow,
In this wild haven, joy will flow.

Nestled in the Wilderness

A squirrel grins with chubby cheeks,
Stealing nuts that play hide and seek.
A rabbit hops with shoes untied,
In this leafy maze, where critters hide.

The tree stump holds a secret joke,
As owls play chess and crows provoke.
Frogs in bow ties croak their tunes,
While the sun lazily snoozes by noon.

Each hidden nook, a riddle spins,
Where laughter bubbles, and mischief begins.
A dance of shadows, a merry chase,
In this wild spree, we find our place.

So join the fun, leave worries behind,
In nature's folly, true joy we find.
With giggles sprouting, let spirits soar,
In this whimsical realm, there's always more!

The Veil of Thorns

A porcupine dons a spiky crown,
Declaring itself the lord of the town.
With thorns as shields, it struts about,
Warding off anyone with a doubt.

Beneath the brambles where laughter roams,
A hedgehog snores in thorny homes.
A snail in a tutu takes the stage,
Performing ballet, it's all the rage.

The thickets shimmer with jokes untold,
As raccoons shine like treasures of gold.
With every twist, a giggle unfurls,
In this thorny jest, nature twirls.

So heed the whispers of mischievous mirth,
As thorns tickle secrets of the earth.
Behind every bough, a chuckle lingers,
In the veils of thorns, joy always zingers!

Shaded Sanctuaries

In the shadows where sunbeams play,
A cat naps tight, dreaming away.
While chipmunks plot their sneaky schemes,
In search of treasures and nutty dreams.

The daisies giggle, with petals so bright,
As fireflies twinkle, flirting with night.
Under leafy bows, mysteries unfolds,
Every shimmer a giggle, stories untold.

A turtle jogs, with a slow-motion flair,
While butterflies twirl without a care.
The joy of shadows, a whimsy spree,
In shaded sanctuaries, we all agree!

So come and dance, my merry friends,
In this haven where humor never ends.
With laughter echoing, and joy set free,
Shaded sanctuaries are blissful glee.

Secrets of the Sun-Dappled Earth

A woodpecker drums a silly beat,
As ants march proudly, tiny but neat.
Each sunny glint holds a prank or two,
In the earth's warm embrace, they're never blue.

A gopher grins, with a mischievous dig,
While frogs throw a party, doing a jig.
Sun-dappled rays break into laughs,
Joining small creatures in playful chaffs.

With toadstools as tables, they feast in delight,
Telling tall tales from morning till night.
The secrets concealed in the sun's gentle breath,
Are simply jokes mocking the fate of death.

So wander along the joyous terrain,
With a wink at the critters, embrace the mundane.
In laughter and glee, let your spirit unearth,
The secrets swirling in the sun-dappled earth!

Where Shadows Linger

In the woods where shadows play,
A squirrel steals my lunch away.
I chase him down, but he's too slick,
He laughs and darts like a magician's trick.

The owls hoot jokes from their high perch,
While rabbits dance in a wild search.
The old tree grins, its bark a frown,
Telling tales of how we all fall down.

When the sunlight dips to hide its face,
I tumble in a bush, oh, what a place!
The thorns and brambles giggle in glee,
As I wiggle out, feeling quite free.

So here's to the woods, with laughter and cheer,
Where shadows linger and nothing is clear.
I'll return for more chaos, in glorious fun,
With squirrels, owls, and shadows on the run.

The Buried Beneath

They say there's treasure buried down low,
But first I dug a hole for my toe.
With spades and shovels in clumsy hands,
We searched for gold in dirt mounds and sands.

We found a shoe and a rusty key,
A map that led us straight to a tree.
The map was pointless, or so it seemed,
It's just a bird's nest, where a crow dreamed.

Yet laughter erupted with every flop,
As we tumbled and rolled, we just couldn't stop.
We buried our snacks beneath all that muck,
And laughed till we cried, what a day—what luck!

So here's to the gems that will never be found,
Like friends having fun, spinning all around.
Forget the treasure, just let it be,
The fondest of riches are wild jubilee.

Crooked Realms

In a land where the wonky trees lean,
And the bunnies bounce like they've just seen a queen.
I stumbled upon a crooked old door,
It squeaked as I opened, 'Not another bore!'

Inside, the floor danced with steps too zany,
Where frogs wore hats, looking quite brainy.
They croaked their tunes with a jazzy flair,
While flowers swayed as if in mid-air.

A snail offered coffee, but it was just slime,
I sipped with a grin, it felt quite sublime.
The laughter erupted, an odd, merry crew,
Forming a circle, oh, how we flew!

Crooked realms where giggles soar high,
Are the best of places, I'll tell you why.
For in the oddities, joy does abound,
Leaving straight paths far behind, homeward bound.

Enchanted Shadows

In enchanted shadows where giggles reside,
A fox in a hat takes me for a ride.
With rabbits in bowties, they whisk me away,
To such silly realms where all shadows play.

A dance on the grass with shoes made of leaves,
While rumbling echoes of laughter deceives.
The mushrooms join in, they wiggle and jive,
All in good fun, oh, how they thrive!

From twilight to starlight, winks shared with glee,
I twirl with the shadows, just let it be free.
With every cackle, the night spins anew,
In this madcap world, the fun's overdue!

Enchanted they say, but it's just plain absurd,
Where nothing is serious and all joy's preferred.
So join in the laughter beneath the crescent moon,
With shadows and friends, we'll be back very soon.

Microcosm of the Silent Sanctuary

In a shade where the squirrels play,
The raccoons dance at the end of the day.
A snail stole a hat for a grand parade,
While crickets chirp jokes, totally unafraid.

A rabbit runs fast with a sandwich in paw,
He trips on the roots, oh what a flaw!
The owls all hoot, trying not to laugh,
As the turtle provides a slow-motion gaffe.

The chatterbox birds gossip above,
About sly foxes and a tight-knit hug.
While ants plan a feast for the annual fair,
All while disguising in their best tiny wear.

In this space, all mischief knows no bounds,
With laughter and giggles echoing around.
A playful mix of nature and cheer,
In their happy world, nothing to fear.

Stories from the Understory

Under leaves, where oddities meet,
A frog in a suit has a dance with his feet.
"Jump high!" he sings, to a snail in a tie,
Who responds with a swirl and a mortified sigh.

A hedgehog tells tales, all prickled with fun,
Of marathons run and pancakes well done.
His friends all gather, with chuckles and sighs,
As they roll on the ground, eyes wide in surprise.

In the shadowy nook, where the mischief does brew,
A raccoon wears glasses, and claims he sees through.
"Let me read you," he says, with a pitiful grin,
"Mice tales of cheese, where no tail has been!"

They giggle and snort, in this playful abode,
Where stories are spun and imagination flowed.
In the depths of the wild, they all sit and plot,
A kingdom of laughter, happy and hot.

Shadows Whisper

In the cool of the day, where shadows unite,
A grasshopper leaps, what a comical sight!
He tells of a ghost, who lost his own shoes,
And dances on air, spreading ridiculous news.

Through the branches, the whispers combine,
With the laugh of a crow, and a jolly old line.
Each shadow is shaped like a jester in play,
As the critters all giggle at night turning gray.

The moon winks down, with a playful bright glance,
As a raccoon starts a most peculiar dance.
He says, "If you want to be sly and be quick,
Just wiggle your tail and do the old flick!"

In the hush of the dark, where mirth softly glows,
The stories keep coming, as the night wind blows.
The forest is chuckling, it's truly absurd,
As shadows share secrets, without a single word.

Secrets of the Wild

In the secretive woods where mischief unfolds,
A badger plays poker, with cards made of gold.
He bluffs with a grin, and a chuckle to boot,
While the otters all cheer, ready to scoot.

The whispers of leaves tell wild, funny tales,
Of cats on surfboards, and kangaroos' sales.
Each creature has dreams as big as the sky,
With bats in their capes, they prepare to fly by.

A lizard in shades, lays back with a smirk,
Sips dew from a leaf, enjoying his work.
The critters convene for a fabulous feast,
Bringing snacks made of berries, a delightful beast.

In this wildy realm, where the laughter runs free,
Every corner holds jokes, waiting to see.
So come take a peek at their whimsical ride,
Where the secrets of nature refuse to divide.

Stages of Green

In spring, the sprouts wear hats of dew,
While rabbits giggle, feeling brand new.
Leaves dance around like they own the floor,
While worms serenade with a squishy encore.

Summer brings a heat that's hard to bear,
Grasshoppers strut, without a single care.
The sun beats down with a flaming grin,
As ants march on, planning their next win.

Autumn swirls in with a crisp, silly breeze,
Squirrels stack acorns with whimsical ease.
The trees shake off their coats, big and bold,
While pumpkins tell jokes, or so I'm told.

Winter tiptoes in, all frosty and white,
Snowmen wear shades, in a festive delight.
Nature snores softly, all tucked in tight,
While critters conspire for a springtime flight.

The Darkened Veil

A shadow creeps, with a comical sway,
Pitch-black pants and a hat gone astray.
With eyes like emojis, all wide and round,
It trips on its cape, flops flat on the ground.

Trees gossip softly, but oh, what a scene,
A bat in a tux, looking quite keen.
'Is that a walrus?' a squirrel asks in cheer,
And the veil just chuckles, 'I'm too cool for fear!'

A mist so silly, it swirls and it spins,
While shadows make faces and giggle with grins.
An arboreal party, oh, what a sight,
As specters do a conga into the night!

In the thickness, laughter fills every nook,
As ghouls swap tales straight from a comic book.
When darkness calls, it brings quite the jest,
In the land of the quirky, the spookiest fest.

Solace in the Thicket

In a cozy corner, where the wild things play,
Lies a hedgehog known for a very odd sway.
With a tiny top hat and a bow tie so neat,
He hosts tea parties that can't be beat!

Bunnies with top hats sip tea from a leaf,
Discussing their fashion, sharing their grief.
'Oh dear,' one squeaks, 'I think I have lost,
My favorite carrot, what's the cost?'

Meanwhile, a fox tells the best of his jokes,
While the birds crack up, clearing their throats.
'Thick it may be, but oh, what a laugh,
In this thicket of solace, we share our paths!'

Every rustle and giggle tells tales of delight,
While the thicket embraces all shades of light.
With harmony echoing from critter to critter,
Even shadows join in, flashing their glitter.

Zones of Silence

In a quiet glade where the sun likes to peek,
An owl tells stories, quite odd and unique.
'The moon's in a turtleneck,' he hoots with a grin,
While the hedgehogs snicker, their laughter a din.

Then comes the rabbit, with secrets to share,
But all he can muster is a floppy ear stare.
'This moment is zen!' he declares, wide-eyed,
While the trees just nod, feeling quite dignified.

A turtle's slow dance sends a ripple of peace,
As chipmunks debate if their nut stash should cease.
In the zones of quiet, each giggle's a sound,
And nature orchestrates fun all around.

From buzzing of bees to the rustling leaves,
The laughter ascends, and the heart truly believes.
Although silence reigns in a curious twist,
The whispers of joy are the ones to persist.

www.ingramcontent.com/pod-product-compliance
Lightning Source LLC
Chambersburg PA
CBHW072138200426
43209CB00050B/117